A FILMMAKING

MINDSET

THE NEW PATH OF TODAY'S FILMMAKER

Published by Indie Film Factory, LLC
3111 South Valley View Blvd E-127
Las Vegas, Nevada 89102

Note: The information provided in this book is presented for educational purposes only. The authors are not giving any legal or financial advice. Readers should always consult with the appropriate legal and financial professional prior to making any business decisions. The Publisher, or authors are not liable for how readers choose to use this information.

ISBN: 978-0-578-72399-0

In Memory of our beloved pup Abbey. We shall always be grateful for the time you gave us and the happiness that you blessed our hearts with. We miss you girl.

TABLE OF CONTENTS

A Filmmaking Mindset

By Kelly Schwarze

A person should set his goals as early as he can and devote all his energy and talent to getting there. With enough effort, he may achieve it. Or he may find something that is even more rewarding. But in the end, no matter what the outcome, he will know he has been alive.

—Walt Disney

Introduction:

An Awakening

Why I Wrote This Book

My main goal with this book is simple: I hate bullies. I spent my childhood running from them. In fact, one of the main reasons I am in a creative field is because I spent most of my adolescence hiding from the circumstances of my early life. Art was my form of escape, and it gave me a sense of being. As I became an adult and ventured deeper into my filmmaking career, I discovered a new front line of bullies. This time it was not the mean kid on the playground or the gang on the basketball court. These days, bullies come in the form of industry leaders, distribution executives, and online critics. Even worse, creatives often bully themselves because of their lack of self-confidence and their misunderstanding of the business world around them. This said, I believe there is something that can be done. You can develop a mentality that is stronger than criticism, stronger than the obstacles, stronger than money, and more powerful than knowledge or skill itself. For the purpose of this book, this mental strength is called "a filmmaking mindset."

My goal is to help readers stay the course with their filmmaking dreams. I aim to prove that a person can make movies, documentaries, short films, and other media with the resources that they have now and use this moment as a starting point to build a meaningful creative career. You do not need to attend an expensive film school or win the best film at a prestigious film festival to be successful.

One of the biggest hurdles filmmakers face in this business is navigating industry myths and self-imposed dogmas about how movies should be made and what makes them successful. A person can spend a lot of money and time chasing dreams and circumstances that they have very little power over. *Waiting for Hollywood or some film festival to give you permission to be successful is bologna.* You can make a career as a successful filmmaker without a studio backer or film festival accolade. You do not need any sizable amount of money to get started developing yourself as a filmmaker. All you need are a focus point, a plan of action, and an unwavering passion to tell stories.

Who Is This Book For?

Although the information in this book can be applied to any level of film project, this text is largely designed for readers that are making a feature-length movie within the budget range of $30,000 to $60,000. One should be able to produce a solid, quality movie at this range without having to mortgage a home, steal things, sleep under bridges, or be reluctantly forced to call in favors. This information is intended to help every reader develop himself or herself as a filmmaking entrepreneur. You should be able to do so with limited start-up capital.

Throughout this book I will touch upon screen writing, directing, story development, production, and distribution through the filter of a start-up company. This means that you should approach your movie project in the same manner as you might start a new company. You can do this by doing market research, putting together costs and budgets, and creating a plan for growth and long-term success.

Inside This Book

Within the pages of this book, I will cover the following basic conversations and aim to create a new level of thinking for you as the filmmaker. Readers may not agree with all of my ideologies, but be assured that my main purpose with this information is to help one bring structure and order into their careers as cinematic entrepreneurs.

1. Understanding the filmmaking mindset
2. Filmmaking traps and how to avoid them, dispelling myths, and placing confidence in your vision
3. Finding a pathway to success from day one of your development process
4. Exploring genres
5. Creating a physical plan of action
6. Understanding the business of microbudget filmmaking
7. Making a movie for $30,000 or less
8. The importance of casting fewer people
9. Working with a smaller crew size
10. Building your distribution plan
11. Staying on track

How to Use This Book

A Filmmaking Mindset is a companion text to my last book, *What Film Schools Don't Tell You.* In that book, I highlight a step-by-step process to developing, producing, and distributing your microbudget film. Although I will cover most of these topics in some fashion within these pages, this book will focus primarily on the mentality of developing and producing microbudget movies. It is also an important reminder of ensuring cast and crew safety and being organized on set. After you complete this book, I would encourage you to check out my last book and apply both sets of information into your business plan.

More than ever, now is the time to make movies and streaming content, but having a business mindset is very important. There is a content creation gold rush happening, and we are at the center of it! By knowing where to pan for gold, filmmakers will greatly increase their chances of finding industry success. By narrowing one's direction, sharpening focus, and making tiny strategic steps forward, a person can avoid so many of the pitfalls that ruin dreams and goals.

Nothing great can come out of writing a script that no one will read or making a movie that will never pay back the cost of making it. That said, it's not always about making money, but some level of commercial success is necessary for long-term growth. Use this book as a mental guide, and use it to help you develop a different ideology toward your craft as a filmmaker. This book is here to help you develop a *filmmaking mindset*.

Chapter 1:

A Filmmaking Mindset

Why do you want to be a filmmaker? What is your "movie goal"? What types of movies do you want to make? How do you see yourself as a creative entrepreneur? Have you ever stopped and asked yourself these questions? They appear to be simple questions, but a vast majority of first-time filmmakers struggle to have clear answers for themselves. For some, being a filmmaker is about the technical aspect of the process: the cameras, visual effects, editing, or gadgetry. For others, it's about dreams of being famous, rich, or iconic. For a few, it could simply be the urge to tell one single story. There is no wrong answer here, but whatever the reason, you have to ask yourself another fundamental question: "Do I have the mindset to be a filmmaker?"

Over the years I have worked with hundreds of filmmakers, producers, and directors, and one of the biggest challenges that I see in most young (and even some experienced) filmmakers is their inability to make decisions and compromise. Oftentimes, content creators will hem and haw and nitpick at the smallest of details surrounding their ideas. They will wait for conditions to be perfect before making moves. They will edit and edit forever and never release anything. I have seen people take years to edit and release their movies while the world around them changes. Once they do release their movie, the subject has become irrelevant. Sadly, most people, if they actually make a feature-length movie, will only make one in their lifetime. The hardship, patience, and dedication it takes to make a single feature-length film is so enormous that most folks simply cannot subject themselves to a second dose.

The key to a filmmaking mindset is simplicity, understanding that the idea you have now can be told in a multitude of ways. Ideas will come and go, and they will transform and morph into other things. This is OK and is completely normal. The more adaptable you become in your thinking, the freer and more productive you will be. The more productive you are, the more likely you will continue as a filmmaker. It is important for you to seize upon the moment of discovery and make a dedicated effort to see your ideas through. However, your ideas may not always be the perfect rendering from your imagination, but what is important is your action to step forward!

Goals—and movie projects, for that matter—are the same as fitness. The more you practice, the better you are, the better you feel, and the more composed you become. Money can only help you so much. You can have the finest fitness equipment in your house, but if you are not dedicated to using it each day, then you will see no results. Moreover, it is not required to have state-of-the-art fitness equipment in your house in order for you to exercise. You can exercise in hundreds of ways, some of which do not require the use of specialized fancy equipment. The key here is action, not circumstances.

I have spent my entire adult life making moves. Not all of my films have been successful in terms of return on investment (ROI), but the one thing I am most proud of is that I have never given up. I have learned how to cut my losses when the time is right and have been able to compartmentalize my career into stages. I have discovered that my overall success is not contingent on my mastery of the cinematic language, or what the critics say, but rather a particular mindset. It is the same mindset that I have witnessed in entrepreneurs, celebrities, and other people who have achieved success. It's a mindset of always moving forward and making no excuses.

Walt Disney once said, "The way to get started is to quit talking and begin doing." He never dwelled on the problems but on the end results of his dreams. Oprah Winfrey is another case example. Starting from a troubled past with very little opportunity, she set her sights on doing things big and doing things her way. During her early career, trash TV was in its prime, and despite being advised to take the low road to procure higher TV ratings, she stayed the course with her own vision of daytime television, catapulting her into the history books and inspiring millions of people all over the world.

Doing the best at this moment puts you in the best place for the next moment.

—Oprah Winfrey

What Is the Filmmaking Mindset?

A *filmmaking mindset* is not very much different from other business motivational ideologies. It is, in essence, the notion that one can achieve their desired dreams as long as they are willing to put practical plans into effect and focus on the end result. A filmmaking mindset is all of that plus the combination of understanding your limitations and strengths and creating a plan that will promote long-term creative productivity. This mindset starts with knowing and visualizing the outcome of your movie goals, and then creating an adaptable and practical guide in getting to that goal. I use the terms *adaptable* and *practical* because you must have plans that can easily be altered from time to time and plans that are practical within the limitations of your environment.

To master this mindset, one must be able to be adaptable from time to time and work harmoniously with the real world without losing their way or throwing a temper tantrum on set when things don't go to plan. Clint Eastwood famously once said, "I don't believe in pessimism. If something doesn't come up the way you want, forge ahead. If you think it's going to rain, it will."

A filmmaking mindset waits for no one. It does not ask for permission or forgiveness. This ideological way of approaching your career also does not wait for the circumstances or conditions to be good. With this mindset, you create your own circumstances. Napoléon Bonaparte was advised by his generals that the circumstances of battle were not right to advance his attack. He quickly replied, "Circumstances? What are circumstances? I make circumstances."

When I first started my career, I was like most people. I had a vision of what I wanted for myself but wasted time trying to motivate others. I lost valuable time trying to inspire business partners and colleagues, most of whom were more interested in the social status of filmmaking. I quickly discovered that I was continuously moving uphill with people. I was constantly waiting for others to take things as seriously as I had.

After several years of frustration and missed opportunities, I discovered something. I realized that the only person who had the power over my growth was me. I was the only person responsible for my failures and successes. If I wanted advancement in my career, I had to take massive steps forward, whether people were with me or not. I started to understand the value of being the master of my own progress and paying less attention to what others said or thought. My motto became, "The train is moving. You are either on or off."

Las Vegas in the early nineties was a tough place if you wanted to make movies. It was not like today, when you have access to premier filmmaking equipment and resources. If you wanted to be a filmmaker back then, your best odds were moving to Los Angeles or New York. Even more challenging was the fact that there were few affordable film schools around, so opportunities to learn were nearly impossible. Oh, and the internet had not been invented yet!

At the start of my career, I was handicapped with a lack of education, zero finances, and a massive void of mentorship. I went through several years of hardship and emotional struggle until I started finding work-arounds for my career advancement. Luckily, I had one thing going for me: I knew what I wanted to do with my life. The trick was getting there.

I am not embarrassed to admit this, but growing up, I was a hero worshipper. Although my family is filled with wonderful people, their lives were not what I wanted for myself. I had to look elsewhere for inspiration and guidance. I needed a mentor, even if it meant picking one who was dead!

If the quote at the beginning of this book wasn't a clue, I spent most of my early career trying to emulate the likes of Walt Disney. In my humble opinion, his career is at the pinnacle of business achievement and human innovation. For me, Walt Disney's story represents freedom from Hollywood and human perseverance. Although some may call him controversial today, Walt Disney embodies the American dream like no other. He came to Los Angeles a failed and broke entrepreneur, uncertain of his future. He desperately wanted to be in the entertainment business but lacked the capital and industry connections. Even worse, he battled the mental scars of an abusive childhood and suffered from depression. With the support of his brother Roy and countless others, Walt slowly built an entertainment empire brick by brick, without the collusion of any major Hollywood studio. By the time of his death, he *was* Hollywood. His movies entertained children all over the world and touched the hearts of generations to come. Hate him or love him, one thing is indisputable: Walt Disney started with very little, yet he changed entertainment forever.

For the entrepreneur, there is no greater importance in finding a person, whether dead or living, to study and model your career after. There is nothing wrong with being inspired by someone or modeling your life in some fashion based on that inspiration. Without the proper understanding of what you aim to be like, you cannot truly create a plan to achieve success.

Our industry is filled with perseverance stories. Francis Ford Coppola, Brian De Palma, Steven Spielberg, Walter Murch, and George Lucas all came at a time where studios were dominated by old men, yet they managed to rewrite the story and change the industry forever. John

Singleton proved in the nineties that cinema was about to change forever with new voices from underrepresented communities across the world. Kathryn Bigelow, Sofia Coppola, Lucía Puenzo, and countless other women throughout the industry's recent history have challenged the status quo and have brought brilliant works to the screen. All of these examples are people who never asked for permission or apologized for trying.

The Kid from Vegas

Like anyone, your childhood shapes who you become in some way. As adults, we spend a great deal of time trying to reprogram ourselves for the better. For me, it was no different. The emotional driver behind my desire to make films comes from an early age. My childhood was not horrible, but it came with emotional and financial hardships that shaped my early impressions of life. Finding outlets to escape and express myself was important. I turned to drawing and storytelling as my therapy.

When I was around the age of eight, my family was in turmoil. My father had a small manufacturing business, which he mismanaged beyond saving. Due to his alcoholism and a series of bad financial situations, my father's business ultimately closed and forced my parents to file for bankruptcy. Even worse, my parents divorced shortly thereafter, setting off a family feud that would last for decades.

My kid sister and I were uprooted from our family home and moved into a small shabby two-bedroom apartment with our mom. Mom raised us without any support from Dad or our family. The financial and emotional hardships were always present, and life was dramatically different from what we previously had been used to.

Mom was the only breadwinner. She did whatever it took to keep the creditors away and a roof over our heads. Since money was always sparse and going out for movies was a luxury, we watched a lot of VHS movies from home, and a majority of them were animated movies.

I would spend most of my summers watching Disney classics, trying to figure out how things were done. Unable to afford cable TV, I would crash at my friend's house over the weekends just to watch the Disney Channel and Nickelodeon. One particular program I remember watching was a backstage tour of Walt Disney Animation Studios. The program was an in-depth documentary that took viewers on a behind-the-scenes look at the animation process and the artform of visual storytelling. The program made such an impression on me that I decided to dedicate my life to becoming a Disney animator.

The dream of working for Disney came to a head shortly after I graduated from high school. Lacking the funds and the high-level life-drawing skills needed to pursue the art, I was rejected from nearly every animation school I submitted to, except for one school in San Francisco. Unfortunately, the cost of living in the Bay Area was equally restrictive, and I ultimately had to withdraw from that program and return to Las Vegas.

Dejected and lost, I decided to take film studies classes at my local university. Little did I know at the time, my limitations were slowly becoming my greatest benefit. One particular day, I met a man named Michael Berk while working at my day job. Mr. Berk just so happened to be one of the creators of the TV series *Baywatch*. He was also on the board of directors of a local film festival. I told him about my aspirations of breaking into the entertainment business, and he connected me with the festival director. I immediately volunteered and spent the next several months running errands and meeting other filmmakers. In doing so, I was exposed to some amazing people, mostly those who had carved out careers for themselves without formal education.

One such self-made person I met was a man named Gerald R. Molen. Mr. Molen was a major producer who had moved to southern Nevada after the Northridge earthquake in 1994. He had worked with Steven Spielberg on multiple projects, including *Schindler's List*, which won the Academy Award for best picture. Mr. Molen was so generous with his time and made a point of offering me insight into his own success. Like most of his contemporaries, he had worked his way up through the ranks of Hollywood and ultimately landed the top job of producer on several major films.

One of the biggest lessons I learned from talking with Mr. Molen was that there was no correct path to achieve success, especially in the movie business. In fact, the general consensus from most successful people I met was that you had to just do it. You cannot wait for a break. You have to create your own opportunities! Never wait around for someone else to do it for you. You have to make content as if your life depended on it. Never look back and never apologize for trying. And never give a flying crap about what online critics and nasty customers think of you! In the end, the world is never written by critics, only those who have been criticized.

The Money Mindset

Once the rubber hit the road in my career, it became completely clear that funding would always be my greatest challenge. In fact, money challenges are the predominant factor in any level of filmmaking. That said, being resourceful and flexible with your plans are absolute virtues one must have to survive this trade. Not doing something because of money is never an option. You must figure out work-arounds and master the art of doing more with less.

A filmmaking mindset takes all of the normal challenges that face any filmmaker and turns them into opportunities for self-reflection. A filmmaking mindset is about looking past your current conundrums and seeing your career as a lifetime of small and incremental steps toward a larger body of work. Lacking funds to make a film is an age-old problem that never gets easier, even if you find career acclaim. You will always require more, especially as your skills develop and imagination expands. However, if you don't master how to do more with less, you will never move past where you stand right now. *Filmmaking is a balancing act of economics and creativity. The balance should correspond with the realities of the marketplace and what level your career is at.*

I know many people who have spent decades dreaming of making their first feature film. Most of the time, they have no real idea what their dream would cost to make. Typically when asked, "How much would your film cost to make?" people hastily reply "A million bucks!"

Finding a million bucks is no easy feat, and finding an investor who is willing to take a gamble on a first-time filmmaker is even harder. So most people stop there, always dreaming, and ultimately move on to something else. The dream dies, and the story is never told. This is tragic, but it's also completely avoidable.

If you are one of those people who is trying to make your first feature film for a million bucks, I would like to ask you, "Why? What qualifies your first idea to cost that much money? Can you make a thirty-thousand-dollar movie first? Can the overall goal of your story be exposed with this level of budget?" Without even knowing what your content is, I can say with great confidence, "Yes. I'm positive it can!"

Ideas cost very little to produce. It's the baggage associated with the idea that costs the most in filmmaking. Take time to reevaluate your idea and work it into a practical script. If you can do this, you will find freedom. If you can make a feature film for $30,000 or less, then I can guarantee your career prospects will improve tenfold. Not only will you learn how to be resourceful with production hurdles, but you will learn to write for economies of scale. Being resourceful is key to your filmmaking career. You'd better learn to master it.

Chapter 2:

Filmmaking Traps

Before we dive into the tips to help you make a small-budget film, it is important to outline a few traps that most aspiring filmmakers fall into. Oftentimes, novice filmmakers are caught up in the linear portion of the process. People will find themselves chasing the expensive camera brands or allowing existential hurdles (such as money) to stifle their ability to move forward. Even worse, some aspiring creators get into this business for the sake of being cool, or the "prestige factor." This is a surefire way to ruin yourself financially and bring almost certain displeasure to your life.

The Hard and Sad Reality

Another motivation in writing a book like this is to point out a very tragic fact. A very small percentage of people entering the field as directors and producers actually stay in the industry into retirement. The transience of our industry lies mainly in the reality that filmmaking, like most entertainment enterprises, is a speculative business. The industry has little infrastructure in place to measure true success, making it difficult to gauge what works and what does not. Unlike making a house or automobile—processes in which the end result is measured by design, efficiency, safety, functionality, and demand—movies and media are subjective, meaning that each potential customer has their own opinion. With so much content out there to consume, it also makes it difficult for smaller productions to find enough support to gravitate to a level of financial successes, even if the movie is good. However, before we even talk about being a filmmaker, before we even touch a single piece of material or advice I've given to you, let's talk about what stands in your way—what the battle really is!

Things Cost Too Damn Much

I'll never forget meeting a filmmaker who had shot his first feature film for a million dollars. He did so without any previous experience or understanding of the marketplace. He created a religious satire that fell dead on arrival and was lost to obscurity. The movie itself was funny and well produced, although the cost of the film's budget was so stifling that it became an unmanageable burden. The filmmaker has not made another film since.

As with any new business, starting small and working efficiently is the best advice one can give. In today's indie filmmaking world, *keeping your budgets as low as possible will be crucial to your long-term success.* Forget about the million-dollar budgets. Forget about the hundred-thousand-dollar budgets. If you desire to build your business as an independent filmmaker, try to stay under the hundred-thousand-dollar-budget range for as long as you can.

The Cool Factor

In my opinion, the biggest trap for independent filmmakers is what I call the "cool factor" of filmmaking. The cool factor is when the grandeur of the moviemaking process overshadows the storytelling and economics of the business. For some, it's more about how cool they look on set or the selfie they take with the big lights and cameras for their social media profile. The cool factor is about bragging to colleagues about how big their budget is/was. To this extent, the filmmaker is more concerned about his or her own image than making a product that will cost very little to produce and that will work in today's complicated marketplace. This is why many projects fail to start production or find financing.

Not Understanding the Marketplace

In today's ever-changing motion picture business, it is superimportant to understand how movies are developed, how products are sold, and how to create ancillary value from everything that you do. These days, it is much more than making a good movie, getting into a film festival, and praying you sell it to a distributor. Today's industry calls for resourcefulness, thinking outside the box, and an in-depth understanding of economics, marketing, and global audiences.

For the aspiring independent filmmaker, it is overwhelming enough trying to make a movie, let alone think about marketing, distribution, or economics. However, if you start your film project with the mentality of a movie studio executive, you will save yourself countless mistakes and position your film(s) for the best possible outcome. I am hoping that by the time you complete this book, you will have a better perspective on the business and develop the mentality of an entrepreneur. I have written more extensively about this in my previous book, *What Film Schools Don't Tell You.*

A Messy Kitchen

I once heard a chef say, "If you are messy with your kitchen, you're most likely messy with your life!" This is a very true statement. I have noticed over the years the value of being in good organizational health. Not only is being clean and organized good for your mental state, it frees up valuable time to do other things that are more productive. Now, I'm certain there are some readers who are saying, "I'm an artist. I thrive in chaos." This may very well be true for most creative people, but the second the script or idea is out of your head and onto the page, the process is no longer a creative one. The entire situation moves from being a creative work of art to making an industrial product. Production calls for order, planning, cleanliness, safety, and organization.

Cleanliness may be contradictory for many artists who fancy themselves in the image of the creative recluse who lives on the edge but is perceived as brilliant. This theory may work for poets, sculptors, musicians, painters, or songwriters, but it doesn't fly for the modern filmmaker who requires multitudes of people, coordinating efforts, schedules, cash, and other moving parts to complete a relatively expensive product. Moreover, in order to attract funding and support for a project, the filmmaker needs to inspire people with his or her work ethic. Being organized in your life is a great place to start.

If your car is messy, then your production will be messy. If your home is messy, then your set will be messy. If you are unkempt or unhygienic, then the health of your production will follow suit. I cannot stress this point enough. You have to change this part before you can effectively lead an army of people to the task of filmmaking. Being clean and organized is a key attribute to any financial or business success.

Those Old Filmmaking Myths

I must conclude this chapter by dispelling a series of old filmmaking myths. There are plenty. Most of these myths are promoted by film-school programs and film festivals that are still operating in a pre–video-on-demand (VOD) era. Most of these myths point to the outdated idea that your career as a "filmmaker" can only be valued if you have a major film festival accolade, win gold trophies, or have works that are acquired at a Hollywood level. Now surely those things wouldn't hurt to have, but let me be very clear: you don't need any of it to make your movies or to find commercial success as a filmmaker.

Here are some of the biggest myths out there:

1. You need to move to Hollywood to make movies.
2. You need a film festival accolade to get distribution.

3. Getting into a major festival with your film is the *only way* to guarantee distribution.
4. You always need movie stars and famous people if you want to sell your movies.
5. To produce a quality product, you need to spend a million dollars.
6. You can't do things yourself. You need to hire seasoned professionals in every department.
7. You should only go union.
8. Feature films are the only types of movies that sell commercially.
9. You need a film distributor to distribute your film.
10. Once you find a distributor, your job is done. They will do everything else.
11. Just make a great movie, and you'll be rich and famous.

With each of these falsehoods, there are areas of some reality, which make it very difficult to separate the BS from what is actually helpful. Moreover, film festivals, trade unions, equipment companies, sales agents, and film schools benefit from some of these myths. It is important to note that the movie business is absolutely no different than any other industrial business. It is about supply and demand and creating a product that can appeal to a broad demographic. By reprogramming your thinking, you will find much more freedom and fewer constraints. However, it is true that you need certain things to make your movie and be successful, but you don't need everything that the industry claims you do.

As I digress, I ask you to discard all old ways of thinking when it comes to filmmaking, and allow me to offer you some new theories, perspectives, and directions that will better service you as a creative person. Don't allow yourself to get caught into the "trap" of the filmmaking dream, but rather look at your career as a life journey. It won't always be easy, but if you take one baby step at a time, you will find a long and rewarding career ahead of you.

Chapter 3:

It Starts with Development

Where to Start

Most people I consult ask the basic question, "Where do I start?" This book is here to help answer that question. The filmmaking journey should start with creating a mindset that will protect and guide you through the treacherous indie filmmaking landscape. Secondly, it is vitally important to be organized. By this, I mean having your plan of action in place. Create shot lists, schedules, budgets, and any other tools on paper that can help you effectively execute a movie project. If you have equipment, it should also be organized so you or others can locate things more easily. Clean up your computer files. Organize your scripts and documents into folders. Whatever you can do to make things more orderly, the better.

Not only is being organized as a filmmaker important, but it is also important to be organized in one's personal life; this includes the places you live and work.

Declutter and dejunk—unless, of course, you need stuff for props. However, without some order, some system, or some apparatus to help, an individual cannot effectively focus on his or her creative career. Take some time to organize your life. Dejunk, declutter, and try to clean up your living environment to operate like any other business.

Filmmaking is a business, like it or not, and the same principles apply to success as they do to any career or occupation. Most rational people would not eat at a filthy restaurant. Parents would not hire a babysitter or a pet sitter if they arrived looking like a slob or were a dysfunctional mess. Crew people won't want to work with a director or producer who don't have their act together. Would you?

What Is Filmmaking Success?

The dream of becoming Hollywood's next big thing is alive and well. And while there is nothing wrong with having that goal for yourself, the true key to any level of filmmaking success is having the ability to create regularly and earn money from the work you do. For me, the truest form of my success comes from the ability to work independently from the constraints of Hollywood while still finding commercial success with my work. That said, my movies and projects have made returns, and I have personally received a good number of industry accolades. I have been nominated for several Emmy Awards over the years, including ones for documentaries and commercials, and finally took home one Emmy in 2020 for a PSA I produced for the Nevada Film Office. Additionally, my feature *Abigail Haunting* was in the top ten most popular movies on Amazon Prime for several weeks and has been seen by people all over the world. All of my films have worldwide distribution and have been translated into multiple languages. So for me, I feel that I have accomplished several things that by industry standards would be considered success. Nonetheless, I feel as independent as ever!

Despite not having the support of a major studio or windfall of capital investment, I set out every two years to produce a feature motion picture. I do so on these basic principles:

1. Make a movie I would enjoy watching.
2. Tell a story from a simple and singular perspective.
3. Make a film with a superior production quality.
4. Integrate convincing acting.
5. Make a movie that easily can be marketed in one of the nine popular buyer genres: action, sci-fi, thriller, drama, comedy, horror, family, holiday, and romance.
6. Make a movie that can be effectively produced for a budget range between $30,000 and $60,000.
7. Make a production that can be completed in twenty days or less.

Each year my team and I meet to discuss ways we can develop content that can be managed on smaller budgets. *Working on a smaller budget does* not *mean a reduction of quality.* This is a point I must stress. Regardless of whether your budget is fifteen million dollars or fifteen thousand, the overall production quality (i.e., story, acting, camera, sound, and lighting) must be acceptable for general audience consumption. This ultimately means that your movie must sound good, look good, and have convincing-enough actors and stories. My team and I develop our content on a scale of economy, meaning the scope of the project should be consistent with our budget realities. The idea should allow us to produce that scope truthfully and professionally. Here is an example:

The budget: $30,000

The plot: A spaceship crashes on a strange planet where alien life is hostile. One woman struggles to survive while putting the pieces together of her dysfunctional, broken marriage.

In this example the movie is set in the genre of sci-fi. There are several factors we have to ask ourselves:

1. Can this movie look good with the budget we have?
2. Could this story lend itself to a singular location?
3. Would the acting be good enough for a limited cast to perform? (This means there would be only a few actors in the movie.)
4. Can we create a convincing world and drama that fans of this genre will accept?

If the answer is "no" to any of these, then we have to reevaluate the scale of economy with this plot. For instance, it might be too expensive for us to create a realistic spaceship, or it may require too many visual effects to satisfy sci-fi fans with our "alien life." In this case, we may have to look at either working the scope down a little or changing genres. Here are some alternatives.

> **Plot alternative 1 (keeping it in sci-fi):** An isolated research facility on a strange planet where the conditions of life are hostile. One woman struggles to survive while rebuilding her life after a dysfunctional, broken marriage.

In this alternative, we still keep in the genre of sci-fi, but have changed a "ship crashing" to an "isolated research facility." A research facility might be easier in terms of building the set, designing production, or finding the location. Secondly, rather than having a movie that requires us to produce "alien life," where we will have to create creatures or visual effects, we have made the antagonist of the movie about "surviving the environment," in which "the conditions of life are hostile." This could involve quicksand, viruses, weather, starvation, storms, or any other dangerous obstacle Mother Nature throws at a character. In essence, we have created *Castaway*—or The Martian.

Another option for this process is to consider what this same plot would look like if it were in a different genre. Here are some options for each of the remaining genres. Pay careful attention to how we adapted the plot to fit each genre setting.

Plot alternative 2 (horror): An old house in rural Connecticut was the scene of a gruesome murder fifty years ago. A woman quickly finds herself confronted by the home's tormented spirits while putting together the pieces of her dysfunctional, broken marriage.

Plot alternative 3 (drama): After returning to her family's farm, where the conditions between her parents are hostile, one woman struggles emotionally while putting together the pieces of her dysfunctional, broken marriage.

Plot alternative 4 (action): An abandoned bread factory on a bad side of town where the neighborhood is hostile. One woman struggles to survive while putting together the pieces of her dysfunctional, broken marriage.

Plot alternative 5 (family/holiday/romance): A small town in everyday America where her high school crush still lives. One woman returns home to help her family after leaving a dysfunctional, broken marriage, only to find herself fighting off the urge to fall in love again.

Plot alternative 6 (comedy): An insurance office on a Friday afternoon, where the conditions of the job are ridiculous. One woman struggles to get a promotion while hiding her crazy ex-husband in a janitorial closet.

If you notice, the integrity of the plot is still there. In all of these examples, the through line of the story is a woman overcoming some level of romantic or personal struggle. This is the theme. Regardless of genre, the theme remains the same. This is where I believe the birth of a project is born and transforms.

Typically, when I start a film project or concept development process, I look at how I intend to make the audience feel. This serves as my guide throughout the entire process. This helps me stay focused on the main goal and allows me to direct more effectively. Here are some examples of my common motivations:

- To love
- To feel revenge
- To feel like you need to prove something

- To feel trapped
- To feel nervous about your surroundings
- To feel like the chosen one
- To feel loss or lost
- To feel hopeless
- To feel oppressed
- To feel obsessed

With any of these, you can find a circumstance or plot that could help promote that feeling, regardless of genre. If you are developing an action film and choose the emotion "to love," you can easily make this the goal of your main protagonist, all while he or she kicks ass and takes names. These motivations are simple and very universal. Movies are about making people feel things, more so than just showing them stuff. Focus your efforts on how people should feel when they watch your movies, rather than what you are trying to seduce them with visually.

Another point I must stress before moving to the next section is this: do not write your script before you have these elements figured out! Oftentimes, novice screenwriters start a screenplay based on a scene they have in their heads. They write the scene in such great detail, and although it may be masterful, they often are stuck understanding how this one fantastic scene connects to a plot and through line of a story. This is where most writers come down with a case of severe writer's block. Before committing to a script, I "beat-sheet" my stories first and then work out all the logistical possibilities ahead of time. A beat-sheet is a outline that serves as a framework for the story and how the screenplay will advance. Once you do these predevelopment steps, your script virtually writes itself!

Rushing into the scripting process without understanding the basics of production and why development is important is the reason there are so many screenplays sitting in storerooms at Hollywood producers' offices waiting to be read. As an independent screenwriter, you have to think of yourself as a business plan strategist. You have to create a plan and strategy that someone else (or yourself) can actually follow. If your plan is too lofty, too expensive, or too huge for the average indie filmmaker, your hard work in script writing may be filed into the wastebasket.

Chapter 4:

Genres and Themes Matter

Over the last decade, I have written and lectured on the topic of genre extensively. Genre matters in so many ways, but more importantly, genre is a category of cinema that helps the filmmaker curtail their projects into an audience demographic. Not understanding genre, or ignoring it, is like buying a car without a steering wheel. You have to know where you are headed, and you need a tool to help direct you.

The topic of the movie genre is floated around film markets like a list of ten commandments. Filmmakers are told that they *must* create their content in a particular genre in order to be successful. While this is very true when looking at foreign sales for movies, genre is generally misunderstood and misused.

Indie Comedy Is Not Dead, Just Hibernating

For years, filmmakers have been told that indie comedies do not sell. It is true that comedies are much harder to sell in international marketplaces (due to language and cultural barriers), but to place indie comedy on the "extinct" list is unfair. With the advent of technology and maximizing genre fun, filmmakers are finding success with their comedies, even in the most unlikely places. Take, for example, the 2017 indie zombie flick *One Cut of the Dead*, which debuted at a small theater in Tokyo with virtually no stars and a meager budget of roughly three million JPY ($25,000 USD). Despite the challenges of mixing horror and comedy, the movie earned fame and prestige. One of the main reasons this movie succeeded, in my opinion, is because the filmmakers knew their audience very well and picked a genre class that would be conducive to a microbudget comedic horror film. More importantly, rather than reinventing the wheel, they simply redressed the subgenre with fresh faces and a different take. The brilliance behind this movie is that it markets itself and can be easily aligned with other popular like-minded comedies such as *Shaun of the Dead* and *Zombieland*. This was very smart, considering that their audience base helped champion the marketing. This type of strategy could be applied to any genre really, but what these filmmakers did so well was that they knew their audience.

Thinking about Your Audience

The main job of any product manufacturer is to think about the audience they are hoping to serve. A person cannot honestly market animal products to people who don't own pets. People cannot expect vegetarians to enjoy their steakhouse unless they have something on the menu for them. Filmmakers have to start their development process zeroing in on who their audience is, what they want, how they think, and what types of things they love. From there, they direct their passion toward those behaviors and create within the lines of their customers. The more specific they are, the better.

Finding Relevant Topics, Not Current Events

Back in the early 2000s, I had a web-based comedy sketch series called *Smidgits*, which parodied current events in an SNL-style fashion. We had a few hits and were mildly successful in the scope of online videos. However, despite the success, it was an exhausting process. We were constantly chasing topical subjects in the news and trying to find relevance. The biggest issue our writing team had was that within a week, the topics of our videos were oftentimes irrelevant. Our window of opportunity per video was very small, and it took a tremendous amount of work each day to stay ahead of it all. Worst of all, we paid for the series out of our pockets, and none of our videos made any ROI!

After two years of spending thousands of dollars and experiencing many sleepless nights, I'd had enough. I was at a breaking point. For the first time in my career, I contemplated giving up. I felt as if I had tried everything. At that time, I had already made three feature films, which were dismal and unsuccessful on every level. I had hoped that this web-based series would be a turning point, and in some ways it was, especially on an educational level.

The one thing that I discovered through our ambulance-chasing development process with *Smidgits* was that most people are creatures of comfort, and they like things that are familiar. As dynamic and abstract as some of our efforts were, the videos that made the biggest impressions were the simple ones, the stories with powerful morals or strong themes such as perseverance, fear, self-confidence, love, and discrimination. These videos seemed to resonate with audiences and were the most evergreen content we produced. As I digressed from the *Smidgits* series, I realized that I needed to use what I learned from that experience for the feature film process. Once I did, our fortunes slowly started to change.

Drivers and Themes

There is a difference between the driver of a story and the theme itself, and oftentimes filmmakers confuse the two. The driver of a story is the gimmick—the genre, the mechanics—in which the story moves through the three acts. The theme or topic is different. It acts as the soul of the movie and is untouched by the mechanics of filmmaking. Here is an example of the two.

> **Theme:** Racial injustice in Las Vegas.
> **Driver:** A cop in downtown Las Vegas fights a corrupt system after learning the death of a minority teen was covered up by his fellow police officers.

In this situation, the theme of racial injustice could be told numerous ways.

The best methodology of picking topics is to look for subjects that are interesting to you personally and that could be of value to others. We all have things that inspire us, give us joy, and make us laugh, and things that scare the crap out of us. Finding one of those common themes is crucial to your storytelling success.

For example, let's start with the topic of my movie, *Abigail Haunting*. The main theme in this movie was not about a ghost who haunted a derelict double-wide trailer in the middle of the desert, but rather a story of children being taken from their underage mothers. The topic of state-sanctioned child abduction haunted me, especially after having my own child. I could not even imagine having my child taken away from me to be raised by strangers. It was a subject that bothered me, and I wanted to explore its theme in the context of a supernatural thriller.

I was introduced to this topic when I had the opportunity to direct a public service announcement on the subject of the failing California foster care system. It opened my eyes to the systemic issues that plague communities generation after generation. What was most disturbing was the dubious motives of some foster homes, and how some people made loads of money from the state by being professional foster parents.

A few years later, I was reintroduced to another problem while scouting a hundred-year-old mental hospital. During our scout, the staff showed us an old nursery where the babies of incarcerated mothers would be taken after childbirth. Many women had children while living in these types of facilities. Some women were institutionalized during pregnancy, while others were impregnated during incarceration by rape. However, the most troubling reality of it all was that if an underage mother had a child, oftentimes, the baby was taken from the mother and placed into a state-run agency. Many mothers had their children virtually kidnapped from them by the state, never to be seen again. There were horror stories of mothers killing themselves after having their children taken from them.

Being a parent myself, I couldn't even imagine someone taking my child, and so within that horror, the idea of a mother losing her child under force became the heartbeat of our story. Now obviously, we had to make embellishments, and the story was modified many times before becoming what people see on screen today. Nonetheless, the soul of the plot still remains the same: How far would a vindictive spirit go to recoup what she lost—her child?

The point of this section is to illustrate that we chose a subject that is evergreen and not something topical. If we picked a theme that involved a news headline, political movement, or trendy technology, we might find ourselves reduced to obscurity before we completed the film.

Finding Your Story's Soul

There is more than one way to tell a story through cinema. When consulting filmmakers on the topic of developing and budgeting, they often argue that their story cannot be told with a microbudget. Now I will confess, some scripts are special cases, such as war movies, period pieces, or political dramas. All of these types of movies require a certain level of budgetary consideration. In those special cases, I advise the filmmakers to find an established producer with a track record who can champion their project. That goal within itself could take years.

When looking at a script, I try to look at the soul of the story. *What is this screenplay about? What is the message? What is it trying to say?* Many times, the idea is better than the execution. Sometimes simplicity can help a story or plot thrive. Here are a few examples of screenplay ideas that could be reshaped to fit into a microbudget.

The Big Budget Idea

Plot: Two soldiers have to cross enemy lines to deliver a message that will save the lives of thousands of soldiers during the First World War.

Technique: A seemingly one-shot experience, making the audience feel like they are in the movie with the actors, crawling through the mud and the hell of war.

Goal: An immersive experience, showcasing the First World War and paying tribute to a grandfather.

Story message: War sucks. Saving lives today is futile if a war continues tomorrow.

Your Microbudget Idea

Plot: Two soldiers pinned down in a trench while trying to deliver a message that will save the lives of thousands of soldiers during the First World War.

Technique: A seemingly one-shot experience, making the audience feel like they are stuck in the trench with these soldiers.

Goal: An immersive experience, showcasing the First World War and paying tribute to a grandfather.

Story message: War sucks. Saving lives today is futile if a war continues tomorrow.

You'll notice that the goal and story message are exactly the same, but the technique used here is consolidated. By trapping the two heroes in a trench and allowing the "theater of the mind" to play bigger than fear itself, we have saved the production thousands, if not millions of dollars, in production costs. Despite the dynamics of a particular screenplay, the soul of the story is bigger than its baggage.

If you find your budget loftier than your current wallet's realities, then it should serve as an opportunity for an evaluation of the type of movie you are trying to make. Perhaps this one needs more time. Perhaps you can trim it down and make it manageable. Perhaps you can start with a smaller project. One thing I can promise you, however: the longer an idea sits unfunded, the less likely it is that you will stay in this business. You need points on the board. Not tomorrow—now!

The Video Game Approach

Start looking at each project you are wanting to undertake as a level of a video game. Each level will inherently get harder as time progresses, so make your first level a process of learning, training, and growing toward a larger body of work. I have made seven feature films, documentaries, and TV shows. Yet I have a handful of scripts I have developed throughout my career that have not been produced. Of course it pains me to see certain stories economically restrictive, but that does not mean I stopped developing those ideas. Some of them have been redefined and made into smaller-scope movies. Other scripts remain on the shelf for the time being, patiently waiting as I develop into a better filmmaker.

No Money? No Problem!

I never let money, or lack thereof, stop me from progressing. I currently make one movie every couple of years, and I am working toward making more frequent content yearly. For my career it has been about forward movement. There is nothing more tragic to see than people year after year still lost in limbo with their unfunded projects.

Most of the feature movies I have produced and cofinanced are between $30,000 and $60,000. I have found this level of production most rewarding. It has forced my team and me to think in simpler terms and more strategically. I have figured out how to maximize relationships and soft money to keep my budgets low. I have discovered how to use technology to bring up the quality of my movies. I have learned and continue to understand how to write scripts that are impactful, yet producible at a lower cost.

I truly believe that by adhering to a few basic and common sense principles while developing your script, you will set yourself on a path for long-term success. My goal is to keep you from burnout avenue!

You Are the Writer, Dammit!

As you read this book, I want you to imagine me, the author, waking up at five o'clock every morning to pound away at my laptop for an hour. I did this over the course of three months to create the first draft of this book. It wasn't easy, and it's not necessarily something that I would consider number one on the fun list, but the point here was the same: this book wasn't going to write itself!

To be a filmmaker, you *must* learn to write screenplays. You must find the time and implement the discipline to do so. I say this to filmmakers all the time.

To the filmmaker: Your movie won't write itself...write your own script!

To the screenwriter: Your script won't make itself into a movie...make your own film!

Before you can even take the first steps in your filmmaking journey, you must learn the basics of storytelling and script writing. It doesn't mean you will have to be an expert on the subject, but you must learn to craft a cohesive narrative. Hiring or partnering with a scriptwriter is fine, but that will only serve you so far. In fact, the more creative hands you have in the pot, the harder your life will be as an indie creator. Sometimes marriages between filmmakers and screenwriters work out, but for the most part, unless there is some monetary incentive, screenwriters often have a difficult time taking the back seat on indie productions. It is cleaner and less expensive for you to learn the basics and write your own script. From there, you can always hire or bring in a partner to help you shape things up.

The same concept goes for screenwriters who are holding scripts in their hands and asking, "When will someone make my work into a movie?" Just make your own movie. Write something you can produce. You control the clock, the character list, and the entire production with your pen. Why wait for someone to give you permission or to save you? No one will save you or give you permission. You always have to take matters into your own hands.

Now I know a few of the readers of this section may be thinking some of these thoughts:

- What if I'm not any good at screen writing or storytelling?

- I just like cameras and doing visual effects stuff.
- I just want to direct actors.
- I don't have the time to write scripts.
- I trust a professional who has the training.

These previous thoughts are what keep most aspiring filmmakers in bondage their entire careers and are oftentimes why most quit. They either feel as if they should be entitled to only wearing one hat or that they are not good enough at doing something. In both cases, they are fatally incorrect. You will make bad movies; just accept that. You will embarrass yourself; just accept that. You will not be a Greta Gerwig or Bong Joon Ho on your first go. Just get over it and start making mistakes. Experiment, and do not be afraid to fail. Success in this industry is gained by trial and error. You cannot have success without some failures.

Learn to write. Discipline yourself. Make time for writing, and *write things that you can produce in your backyard first!* Work on short films. Experiment with your cell phone. Whatever you can do to get the creative chemistry moving in your brain and onto the screen, do it!

There are several great books and resources out there that can help you learn screen writing. These books include *The Guide for Every Screenwriter*, by Geoffrey D. Calhoun, and *The Visual Mindscape of the Screenplay*, by Bill Boyle. Additionally, take some screen writing or creative writing classes, or join a writers' group. Make this process your first step in development. You can also locate and download scripts from major films. Read them, and see how things are formatted and how dialogue and action are presented.

The same thought goes for anyone who is a screenwriter looking to break into the business. Take some basic video courses; watch some tutorials on cinematography and editing. Start building a small team of supporters, and make your movie! That may sound easier than it really is, and I get it. It can be overwhelming, but the first and most important step is to decide to do it. Take baby steps, and work toward a career of making your own movie. If you can get a few of your scripts to screen to showcase your abilities, think of it as marketing your business as a screen-writing career. What better way to show your writing chops than to actually have stuff made? Just make it yourself. Get things moving. Wait for no one!

Chapter 5:

A Physical Plan of Action

Let's Be Real

There is nothing wrong with dreaming big. But dreams are just that. They are lofty and typically unattainable *until you put a physical plan into action.* Before you can adapt a thinking that will be conducive to the spirit of entrepreneurship, you must ask yourself the following questions:

1. Am I willing to work on my craft and goals day after day without losing interest or getting distracted?
2. Am I willing to make mistakes, learn from them, and move on?
3. Am I willing to invest the rest of my life toward this goal?
4. Is the reward of what I am wanting to do greater than the sacrifices I am making to achieve them?
5. Am I able to face criticism, ill will from others, and brokenheartedness in following my dreams?

Many people make the mistake of thinking that filmmaking is different from other entrepreneurial endeavors. It is not. In fact, filmmaking is no different than someone looking to start a food delivery service, construct a building, or open an online clothing store. The same basic principles apply to making movies as they do to any other developed product, service, or business. However, before anyone can effectively create motion pictures, they must learn and implement the basics of organization, task mastering, and people skills into their life.

It is also important to note that 80 percent of what we do as filmmakers is race the clock. Learning how to manage the clock is a vitally important skill set we cannot overlook. If you are a person who wakes up on time or is never late to meetings, then you should have a good grasp on this one.

As mentioned in the previous chapter, being organized in life is also critical. Keeping your life orderly will help you learn compartmental skills, which are crucial when dealing with problems that arrive on set.

Most of the time, film productions can have multiple problems, and your job as an indie filmmaker is to help isolate the issues before they start affecting other areas of the project. Here is an example.

>   **The problem:** The security guard who will open the gate to your first filming location is running late. What can you do?
>   **The solution:** Use the downtime to brief your crew on the day's schedule, rehearse scripts with actors, build cameras, get makeup and hair started from the truck or car, and start shooting establishing shots.

Obviously, a little problem like this can dramatically affect your day, especially if you have limited time with cast or crew. Nonetheless, you must always expect these types of hindrances and create compartmental contingencies to face them. This way the problem can be mitigated, so it doesn't hurt other areas of your production. The worst thing you can do is panic or create an atmosphere of stress, which is what most first-time (and even veteran) indie filmmakers do.

The Indie Filmmaking Business Plan

Like any business, having a business plan is vital. Without one, or without taking time to break down your script, budget, or production plan, you are flying in the dark. Most creators hate the idea of doing this, but you must push through this early stage. This is especially true if you are directing a movie or are the writer-producer. By doing your own indie business plan, you will be better prepared to mitigate the disasters that will surely happen on your set. I always do my own planning. It helps me make better decisions as a director and producer. It allows me to respond faster to solve crucial problems.

Here are a few elements that should be included in your filmmaking business plan.

1. **Screenplay:** Although there are many ways to write creatively, there is only one proper method by which you should format your script. Use

screen-writing software to format your script. This is important because you will need an accurate page count in order to properly break down your shooting schedule.

2. **Script breakdown:** A script breakdown is a document, or series of documents, that breaks down the physical elements of your script into lists and categories. These lists include cast, locations, props, wardrobe, visual effects, stunts, and special production needs.

3. **Production schedule:** After the completion of your breakdown, create a rough schedule of your production. This should bear in mind reasonable working hours, weather conditions of the season, locations and company moves, as well as any logistical challenges that you have to overcome to move people to and from set each day. The biggest factor in scheduling is the number of pages you can shoot in a single day. Although some scenarios vary, it is reasonable to expect your production to shoot anywhere between three to five pages of

script per day. Stunts and other intricate scenes may take more time, but plan to schedule yourself with this range in mind. Scheduling is also a challenging task. If you must, you can always hire a professional production manager or assistant director to help guide you through this process.

4. **Production budget:** While budgets come in all shapes and sizes, it is important to utilize a proper filmmaking budget template to help minimize the risk of missing important calculations. Filmmaking budgets can also be very complicated, depending on the script and location you are filming in. You need to know what things actually cost based on the location, city, or country you plan to shoot the movie in. If you are filming your movie in Las Vegas, costs may differ from where you are used to. If you are doing stunts or visual effects, or building sets, you must know what each of those departments will need to effectively do their jobs. Speculating on costs can be dangerous, so it is sometimes important to hire a professional line

producer or unit production manager who has experience working with these numbers.

5. **Cast list or character list:** In the event you already have your cast in place, it is always a good idea to have a cast list for your project. This list would not only include a headshot from each actor, but also a short biography, which can be used for marketing and promotional efforts.

6. **Distribution plan:** One of the most difficult aspects of filmmaking is distribution. I will cover this topic more extensively in the final chapter of this book. Nonetheless, having a distribution plan is something that you can create before your movie is even into preproduction. A distribution plan should lay out your strategies for either finding a traditional distributor or how you plan to self-distribute your film (or both) and should also include some thought on how you intend to market your film once it is available.

7. **A list of resources:** Most of us have amazing resources that we don't even think about when we

start planning a movie project. These resources could be in the form of a service, a box of old family heirlooms, a cousin with a helicopter company, a brother with a classic car, or an aunt with an old creepy house. Take inventory of all the things you have now that could be of value to your production. Even the small things may be of massive value. For example, I just happened to know a friend who had some authentic-looking dummies made for his Halloween decorations the year before. The dummies had been made by professional props people for one of the shows on the Las Vegas Strip. He was looking to get rid of them, so I promptly jumped in to save the dummies. Less than a few months later, I was working on a new script and had a scene where I needed a bit more punch. I thought about the dummies and wrote them into the script. That one move saved me hundreds (if not a couple of thousand) in props costs and allowed me to have a realistic visual effect.

8. **One-sheets and conceptuals:** This is the fun part. Having some visual presentation is very helpful for you as a filmmaker. Whether you are pitching your business plan to potential investors or you are using it for internal purposes, the goal of art is to inspire. In today's world of social media, it is crucial to start the conversations with your audience early on. Without the luxury of a studio marketing budget, indie filmmakers must use social media to stand out to the public. One way to do this is craft a clean, contemporary one-sheet or movie poster for your business plan. This is also a great way to inspire others to work with you on your project.

One of the easiest ways to do this is to purchase a royalty-free photo license that fits the tone of your subject matter. From there, use typesetting to put your text over the image. Keep it clean and simple, and use fonts that look like the types of fonts that are being used by the big guys. It is also helpful to do some research on movie posters and emulate the styles of font that work best for your film. Be sure not to get too attached to this early poster art, as it will surely change as you go into production and start working with a distributor. This should serve only as an early step toward showing people the direction and tone of your movie.

9. **Look books:** Look books are basically PowerPoint documents that highlight a brief outline of your story as well as location ideas, particular actor looks, and other creative things that inspire you. Think of this as your multipage vision board, where you can show your team and partners the desired lighting, camera angles, and acting directions in which you wish to go.

In conclusion, be sure to take time on this aspect of development. This will serve as your road map to making your film. Without it, you are flying by the seat of your pants. I use my business plan not as a method to finding money, but as a tool to inspire my team and to keep me on task.

Chapter 6:

The Business of

Microbudget

Before you can truly take on a filmmaking mindset, you must first understand the basics of how this business works. Now, I cover this topic thoroughly in my last book, but I want to offer you a few nuggets of knowledge of how movies are sold and developed at this level. Obviously, there are nuances today that will change how movies are distributed, and I assume that by the time you read this book, the market will have changed dramatically since I wrote this chapter. But the key here is adaptability.

With global markets plunging during the early 2020 coronavirus pandemic, the ways we operate as consumers have changed. Our behaviors have changed. How we consume media has evolved, and entertainment on its face value has turned on its backside. However, as much as a disruptor as COVID-19 was to our global economy, there were significant changes already in progress for motion picture distribution. The pandemic served as the final nail in the coffin for some of the old ways of delivering media to the marketplace. And although there have been (and will continue to be) fundamental changes to our business model as content creators, one thing will remain the same: the need to understand the global audience market.

Film Markets

"Film markets" is a fancy way to say "movie trade shows." If you have ever been to a trade show, you will quickly relate to the imagery of loud, crowded convention spaces, crammed with people and attention-seeking booth vendors all clamoring to show off their latest products. A film market is just the same. Film markets are conventions that take place throughout the year in various cities across the globe. These days, there are even niche movie markets that focus specifically on types of genres, whether they are sports, politics, LGTBQ+, family, web, adult, or horror related. The markets last for days and host big parties and networking events. The main goal of these events is for buyers of programming to attend and to meet with sales agencies or distributors. This is where people sell movies, TV shows, or video content. Although some film markets align themselves with film festivals, the markets' main objective is moving product and rights management.

These days, film markets have achieved crucial status among the film industry. More and more companies outside of Hollywood are making content and looking to make deals. The important thing to note is that anyone can attend these markets, although navigating the terrain has become a skill set within itself. Independent microbudget filmmakers can take advantage of the markets to network and potentially make deals with distributors or sales agencies. The markets vary in cost and take place all over the world. If you have the funds, it might be worth attending at least one in order to understand how the system works.

How Distributors Make Money

Understanding how distributors make revenue is one of the most important aspects to any filmmaking education. Now, things have changed over the years, but knowing how movies are sold can help you craft a better business strategy for yourself. Let's evaluate.

How It Works

In the past, distribution companies or sales agencies made money by selling off bulk numbers of movies to various buyers. They typically negotiated a flat rate for all the movie licenses in the sale. The buyer would then have the right to show, rent, or sell (without limitation) the movies they licensed in their various distribution channels, whether that be on TV, VOD, and/or in actual retail stores. The distributor would usually charge a fee off the top of the money they received and then split whatever was left (if any) with the filmmaker. Unfortunately, most filmmakers would never see a dime from the sales because the distributors' fees were so high that recouping those expenses first made it impossible for anything to be left over.

Distributors made out great. They could fabricate any cost they needed to make sure that the money they had to pay to the filmmaker was incremental at best. Worst of all, film distribution companies were making deals with subdistributors through a loophole in the "granting of rights" clause in their contracts. It allowed companies to exclude all earnings from subdistributors as part of the gross receipts. Here is an example:

> If you "granted" a distribution company the exclusive rights to your film, then they technically owned the content for the term of the agreement. They would "license" the rights to your content to other film sales companies, which would then license to other networks or third parties. The money that was collected in those deals was never specified as "gross receipts" in the original filmmaker's contract and was usually excluded from earning reports back to the filmmaker.

Many filmmakers were left scratching their heads each quarter when getting financial reports. Despite how well their movie was performing, the reports would always leave them in the red with the distributor. In essence, filmmakers were producing free content for sales companies for the privilege of exposure. This form of shenanigans gave the industry a bad name and made many indie filmmakers cynical of the distribution process.

How Things Have Changed

Things changed a few years ago with the advent of video streaming. Filmmakers suddenly discovered the power of self-distribution and were connecting with new audiences all over the world. The traditional distribution market also took a huge hit when home video retailers and video rental stores started going out of business. Buyers were no longer purchasing huge libraries but rather individual movie rights for online platforms and streaming channels. These deals were usually at a fraction of the cost and quickly turned the tables around, giving filmmakers more leverage when negotiating the terms of a deal. Content started to matter again, and the idea of "expenses" in a distribution contract became as old-thinking as VHS.

Distributors today still try to get away with expense clauses in contracts, but it is becoming very rare. The cost of delivery has decreased, and it's harder for companies to justify expenses, especially with digital fulfillment. As expenses went away, the accounting became a nightmare for companies. Little by little, they were forced to do cleaner and less complicated splits with filmmakers.

Today, many distributors will do a flat fee or a split of gross receipts. This makes it easier for accounting and less cumbersome. Distributors and sales agents still bundle movies, but they are finding value utilizing their libraries on their own channels. Many companies are now launching their own streaming services and are monetizing content within movie advertising and subscription fees.

How *Some* Indie Filmmakers Make Money

I can only talk about myself here…

My pathway to success is not a one-size-fits-all scenario. However, I feel it is important to share with you how I manage my operations, only to serve as one potential way for you to build your enterprise. Self-funding a project has become the most important attribute for my company's overall financial growth. By not taking money from an investor, it has allowed our studio, Indie Film Factory, to maintain ownership of our library. This allows us to invest into future residual income channels. My strategy is to create quality genre-driven content that can make its money back in the first two years of its release and then to maintain that ownership well into the future. It's the future earnings that I am most focused on. The best way to think about it is in terms of a real estate investment. You purchase a property. You slowly pay it off, and then hopefully with time, it builds equity or can be rented to someone. Eventually the property is paid for, and you can now enjoy the benefits of residual income from that property. The more properties you have, the more income you make. And although movies have a higher earning potential when they are new, having libraries of content can be a financial benefit, even with aging content.

The biggest aspect to this strategy is keeping my movies under $60,000 and making movies that can be easily programmed into various channels. Our content is also evergreen. We don't date our movies with trends or current events. I keep things neutral and focus our creative abilities on telling good stories with strong themes. We often work within the genres of science fiction, horror, thriller, or drama. Although I love comedy, I have found it to be very difficult to develop and produce on my budget level. Additionally, comedies without the provisions of star power can be difficult for distributors to position for the market. Plus, foreign buyers are reluctant with comedy because it doesn't always translate.

The notion of sticking to the confines of genre may sound lame or even boring to producers, although I have also learned the value of playing within the boundaries and crafting content that makes it easier to sell. One of the greatest joys I have is sharing the material I have produced with others. Without an audience who cares, your movie is reduced to an expensive YouTube video.

Working within Those Natural Boundaries

When you work within the boundaries of genre, you are essentially creating your content in a proven system of order. That being said, genres can be molded, combined, transformed, modified, and created anew, but they are there to serve the filmmaker as a road map to the human experience. There can be no balance, harmony, peace, or beauty in our world without the natural laws of nature and gravity. Those natural laws are what have created the world we live in, whether we like it or not. Subtracting any element of those natural laws would throw our existence into peril.

As inhabitants of this reality, we have all accepted that gravity exists. You don't see too many people getting mad at it or trying to start a petition to get it removed. Gravity is a fact of life, whether we like it or not. We may be able to escape gravity by leaving the planet or periodically defying it through modes of aviation tools, but in the end, the gravitational pull of our planet always wins. The natural laws that guide our existence and expressions as humans work basically the same way. They work regardless of our personality, religion, sex, politics, or economic conditions.

Humans are not as complicated as we all like to think we are. Outside of all the existential and material things we seek, we are fairly simple creatures who have particular primeval needs, fears, passions, and aims. The idea of creating content to service these basic human motivations is, in essence, working with the natural laws. You can fight it all you want, but in the end, nature always wins.

Art versus Filmmaking

Many people confuse what we do as filmmakers with the functions of artists. We may have many artistic touches we put to our films, but in the end, we are making a product that has to be produced on an industrial scale. It is also a product that can only be measured by how it speaks to an audience. If it doesn't have an audience, then it cannot communicate a message. Regardless of whether you have the next *The Shawshank Redemption* or a new Marvel film, if no one sees your movie, then it doesn't really exist.

When I hear people compare their filmmaking careers to the likes of artists, I scratch my head. It makes me want to laugh sometimes. Filmmaking is a very technical and financially driven experience that is mandated by the limits and skills of a community of people working on a project.

A movie at its most artistic stage is the idea and scripting stage. Once the script is complete, it is up to the mechanics of production to deliver on that artistic vision. At the end of the day, the mechanics of production are the same, no matter the script. You need a camera. You need sound. You need locations, actors, catering, manpower, and money.

Filmmaking closely resembles the efforts of the automotive manufacturing industry. Think about it. It is part design, part commerce, part technical, and part functionality. A car and movie on the outside can appear to be an artistic masterpiece, but under its hood it looks all the same. It is a carefully crafted design that follows a strict set of guidelines and natural laws.

I know that this conversation may turn a lot of people off about my position, but in order to develop a filmmaking mindset, you must reverse-engineer your thinking and take a practical look at what you are doing as a creator. Oftentimes, people become so caught up in themselves that their egos or artistic visions will never allow them to get anything done. Even worse, they waste the time and money of so many people and become unempathetic bores. I've seen directors throw fits and shut down production because the sunlight wasn't cooperating. I've heard of actors quitting work because the props department gave them spaghetti instead of lasagna! As much as I understand that everyone has a process in which they perform well, your ego must be balanced between the realities of the workplace, your budgetary means, and the constraints of the natural world.

Chapter 7:

Making a Movie for $30,000

These days, with technology, you do not need as much to make a movie. That is a great thing from a company start-up position. I produce movies on the scale of $30,000 to $60,000. With this budget range, I am able to self-finance most of my content. This offers me control over the product, and it helps me get an ROI faster than some other films. That said, my margin of error is razor sharp, and attention to quality and scale matters. Before I discuss the creative attributes to maintaining quality, I must start with the functionality and mechanics of development and production. Anytime I sit down to make a movie, I think of these following points:

1. Can I make this idea within a fifteen-to-twenty-day period?

2. Can this movie be produced with good acting, sound, camera, lighting, and production design for my budget?
3. Is this a story that can gain attention or help me get my ROI in a reasonable amount of time?

If the answer to any of these three questions is *no*, then I rinse and repeat the process. Before an idea can make it into consideration for production, it has to hit these basic elements. Quality is a high priority to me. I have not always hit the mark with my directing, acting, or story, but the one thing I have always been impressed by is the overall production quality of our pictures. Our sound is top notch. Our camera work, lighting, and sets have always been way above standard. We also spend a great deal of time in our final mix to help elevate the production with great sound design and music. That all said, perfection is something I strive to hit each and every time I set out to make a movie. Although I rarely hit that level of perfection, it is always a good aim nonetheless.

Make the Movies You Can Afford to Make

I will say this twice for you. If you are making a small microbudget movie, only produce the type of movie that you can afford to make. Once again: If you are making a small microbudget movie, only produce the type of movie that you can afford to make.

To clarify the previous statement, one should evaluate their ability to make a movie based on the following criteria:

1. You can afford limited liability insurance and workers' compensation insurances.
2. You can afford to pay for the proper permits and safety requirements.
3. Your movie can be produced within a week or two.
4. The set and production are safe and managed properly.
5. You can shoot your movie within an eight-to-ten-hour window each day and allow time for proper meal breaks.
6. You can pay your cast and crew a monetary sum for their time and efforts.
7. You can properly feed your cast and crew while on set.

8. Your scenes can be filmed practically and safely, without breaking laws or violating the rights of others.

Run a diagnostic of your idea through these filters before spending any time scripting or building props and such. Take time to do a wellness and viability checkup before choosing to go down the road.

Small Page Count Matters

Making a movie for thirty thousand dollars is simple. Making a thirty-thousand-dollar movie that doesn't totally look like a thirty-thousand-dollar movie is much harder. In order to do this, you must start with the number of pages your script has.

We've all heard that a screenplay page represents roughly one minute of screen time. This is mostly true—*but did you know that most filmmakers can only effectively shoot four to six pages of script per day?* That is, if they are experienced and if everything goes correctly.

I've heard of directors shooting ten to fifteen pages of script in a day. Unless they are making a seemingly one-take *1917*-type movie, then it is highly unlikely they are creating any quality camera setups. In fact, I've seen some of these so-called fifteen-page-a-day productions, and they look messier than a kindergartener's refrigerator art! The shots are typically incoherent and rushed, and the attention to sound quality and lighting is a monstrosity. Even more troubling, filming this many pages a day is usually nauseating for performers. Not only do they need to memorize their lines, but they are forced to work overly long days to accommodate such chaos.

Digressing from the previous thought, it should only be your aim to shoot four to six pages within a day. You should keep your days under ten hours. Your production schedules should only be a maximum of twenty days. That said, page count is vitally important to making this scheduling formula work.

Let's do the math:

4 pages x 20 days of filming = 80 script pages

or

5.3 pages x 15 days of filming = 80 script pages

That's right. *Eighty pages.* Eighty pages qualifies your project as a feature film and allows you to produce it under a reasonable amount of time. I typically keep our scripts to seventy-two to seventy-five pages. Not only does this give my schedule breathing room, but it allows me to move things around if trouble arises.

Eighty Pages? This Author Is Crazy!

Now, you may be asking yourself, "How do I just make a script that has eighty pages or fewer? This Kelly guy is crazy!" Well, it is a great question, and yes, I am a filmmaker, so I am somewhat crazy! However, I am willing to bet that most scenes that you have in your script could go on a diet—or be cut completely. I am also betting you could make such script edits without interfering with the integrity of your story.

As a consultant, I read lots of scripts that host tons of expository and disjointed scenes. This fluff typically does not service the theme of these stories. They are usually written into scripts as beats or backstory devices, which slow the pacing down and create more expense on the budget. Less is always more, and if you are trying to produce a movie for thirty thousand dollars, then you better take stock in consolidating your pages.

Without diving too much into the topic of writing, I will offer these simple tips about your screenplays.

1. **Keep it simple.** Think back to when you were a kid. The films that we loved were all very easy to follow.
2. **Cut out the redundant stuff.** If it sounds like we've already said this, then do not repeat.
3. **Don't move around so much.** The more locations your characters have to move through, the more locations your crew and production have to move

through. Location moves are a killer for a microbudget. More on this later.

4. **More cast equals more problems.** If you need more than five actors to tell this story, then go back and reread the section on development. More cast means more headaches for your microbudget. Keep your cast size small!

5. **Stop talking.** Tons of dialogue can drag your movie into a slumber and slow you down completely. Ask yourself, "Can you show this information without having your actors tell it?" If the answer is yes, then figure out a way to show rather than tell. Plus, less talking also means less time you and your crew will waste waiting for the sounds of airplanes to clear.

By adhering to these basic principles, you will discover amazing possibilities with your ideas. It will help you turn your wonderful story into a producible script. This mentality on screen writing will also service you throughout your career, regardless of budget. It will force you to think differently about what is important to telling stories.

Location Moves Will Break Your Back

Every time you and your cast and crew have to pack up and physically move to another location, that is called a *company move*. Let me say this again. Every time you and your cast and crew have to pack up and physically move to another location, that is called a *company move*! Learn this term and commit it to memory, because it is the one smoking gun that will kill the high hopes of any microbudget film endeavor.

The term is so offensive to me that it makes my stomach turn any time I see it on a call sheet or production schedule. Company moves not only cause momentum loss for the production, but they also result in wasted time and money. I see company moves quite often on schedules of consulting clients. I will hear filmmakers say, "But it's only down the street" or "How else are we going to shoot this movie in twenty days?" In each case, the flaw is in the script design.

Screenplays with lots of location changes are a death trap for microbudget productions. Each time you have to pack up, it will cost you roughly two to three hours of productive work time, and it can and will put your production team at unnecessary risk. Now, with that said, company moves are going to happen after you complete a scene at a location. Once you are done, you are done. However, more than one company move within a single day is a poor decision that will inevitably cost you.

I have seen some production schedules where the cast and crew will be required to make four location moves in a day. They will shoot at a house, then pack up, move to a bar, shoot the bar scene, then pack up again and move to another house, and so on. Most of the time this happens because the producer(s) feel they are maximizing cast and crew labor. After all, you pay for things by the day. If you can get more stuff done in a day, why not? Wouldn't that save you money? Well, the answer is a resounding no. It is true that you may be able to maximize your location needs by consolidating everything in a day, but you will more than likely fail at staying on schedule for the day, meaning (overtime) risk, running your cast and crew into the ground, and falling short on capturing quality shots and performances. Moreover, you create logistical stress that is otherwise avoidable.

Allow me to paint a picture to further convince you of this bad production planning method.

I rented our studio, Indie Film Factory, to a production that had its call time at 8:00 a.m. The crew shot at our studio for nearly five hours, then packed everything up, including craft services, makeup, props, and people, and drove out to a house location nearly fifteen miles away. There, they shot for three more hours before ultimately moving again to film at a nightclub downtown. In the producers' minds, it was simple: *Let's hustle and knock all these little location needs out in one day.*

Now, although it may have looked great on paper, the producing team failed to factor in reality! Driving between places, dealing with traffic, and packing things up can take at least two hours or more, depending on the size of your production. This was exactly the situation here. The misguided crew also forgot to factor in lunch.

Once the crew landed at their second location, the team was already starting to mutiny and demand a meal. The producers then forgot to inform the owner that they would need to shoot outside in the driveway, blocking the owner's car. Because of all the rushing around to make their next move, they failed to keep proper communication going. So now it's 2:00 p.m., no one has had lunch (remember, they started at 8:00 a.m.), the cast and crew are getting "hangry," the homeowner is upset, and they are now officially two hours behind schedule.

By 7:00 p.m., the producers officially wrapped the house scene. The cast and crew finally got lunch, but it was a "working lunch," so no one really had a chance to eat and break properly. The team was still moody, and by then they were completely worn out…but guess what? They still had one more location to go to!

Once again, the cast and crew packed up and loaded out all their gear. This time, it took nearly three hours to make the move, and the production team was running dangerously on fumes. To make things more complicated, the club had given them permission to film between 9:00

p.m. and 10:00 p.m. before their business peaked between 10:00 p.m. to midnight. The club was obviously not happy with the producers' requests to move their filming window.

Once the production convoy hit the nightclub location, the cast and crew sat outside for nearly forty-five minutes in a dark, seedy parking lot waiting for the producers to hash out a new deal with the club. After some heated moments and more money paid to the club owners, the production was finally granted access to load in. However, the caveat to all this was that the production could no longer film in the main area they initially desired. They had to accept a small banquet room that was poorly set up and looked like a cheap truck stop. The director was tired, miserable, and unhappy with his location.

In the end, the crew finally finished the shoot around 1:00 a.m. the next day. The lighting and acting was subpar, and the crew was at its breaking point. Later that night (or morning), senior crew members confronted the producers, and a larger conflict erupted. The sound person and lighting grip walked off and quit, causing troubles for the production later in the schedule. To make matters worse, when the production team returned to Los Angeles, they discovered that they needed to reshoot both the house scenes and nightclub shots. The entire second part of the day was worthless.

All of this mess could have been avoided had the production split up its schedule and made the house location a separate day, shot that scene during the daytime, taken a huge break, and then moved to the nightclub in the evening. They still would have had a company move, but the long break in between would have been plenty of time to break the crew for a recharge and logistically move things at a better rate. An even better idea would have been to break all three locations into smaller half days. They would have spent the same amount of money in the long run.

Rushing around is not helpful. Hustling around is not helpful. As a producer, your biggest job is managing the clock and making sure people are safe. As I digress from this story, I use it to illustrate to you the importance of production planning and producing scripts with fewer location moves. When you are writing or looking for scripts, seek screenplays that have a minimum number of locations. Now, I am *not* referring to location changes such as "int. living room," "int. kitchen," "ext. driveway." I am referring to locations that are completely separate environments from one another. If you do have multiple location changes in your script, plan accordingly to minimize headaches for yourself and team.

Chapter 8:

Casting Fewer People

I start this chapter with one phrase: *All Is Lost*. Now I'm not talking about how some of you may be feeling after reading my earlier chapters. No, I am talking about a little-known movie made with Robert Redford back in 2013. The movie is about a mariner who falls asleep at sea and wakes up lost and stranded. The movie, despite having only one actor (Redford), managed to go on and receive nomination after nomination for everything from best sound to best performance. What made this seemingly straightforward narrative so captivating is that it captured the fear, drama, and horror of our imaginations. It accomplished these things within the constraints of one location and with one actor. The movie was a microbudget (by Hollywood standards) and still managed to find critical and commercial success in the market. Now, having the legendary Robert Redford as your only star does not hurt, but in terms of Hollywood, this little movie makes a great case study on why less is always more!

Having the ability to tell stories with as few "spinning plates" (actors, locations, props) is truly a skill set that one must learn to manage to produce a microbudget movie. I would go on to push this point even further by saying that acquiring this skill is absolutely necessary to be a successful filmmaker on any level.

One of the most quintessential traits of an independent filmmaker is their ability to be resourceful. It's the ability to turn your mom's garage into a WWII bunker or a strip mall retail store into a postapocalyptic holdout. Perfecting your storytelling to involve fewer mouthpieces is something you must learn to deal with.

How to Practice

Have you ever played the game charades? Charades is great because it forces the creative side of the brain to make visual cues to objects and actions. This is a vitally important tactic when writing for scripts that call for singular actors and locations. Rather than several actors bantering back and forth, you are forced to tell your story through action and not dialogue. Obviously, you can help your actors with things like talking artificial intelligence (AI), discovered text, or a volleyball with a face, but not having another character for your antagonist to talk to might be tricky. So I encourage you to start playing the game charades.

Cheap Tricks

A great trick in creating a story with small cast sizes and limited dialogue is to show the audience one secret about each of the characters or environments that the main character doesn't know. Allow the audience to see a sliver of information that could hurt or kill our hero. This adds tension and helps keep people on edge.

For example: Joe, our protagonist, comes home from a long day at the office. In a previous scene, we established that he ran out in a hurry that morning and left his oven on with the door open! When Joe comes home that evening, he is completely oblivious to the danger. To make things, worse he lumbers around his apartment, dragging the audience through this highly frustrating experience of not knowing the danger awaiting him. He sets his things down, brushes his teeth, checks his emails, and starts getting sleepy. He never once gets back to the kitchen to see his stove open. This scene could kill poor Joe and could also kill off several minutes of productive nondialogue screen time. As Joe bumbles around doing mundane tasks, the audience is hanging on by a string. This is a technique used frequently in suspense thrillers and horror films: we allow the audience to see a piece of critical information that our hero is ignorant of. Thank you, Alfred Hitchcock! This trick enables the filmmaker to create an effective scene without the hubbub of multiple characters interacting or of dialogue. You could easily build more tension with some foreboding music and sound design.

Trapped or Lost

Whether our hero is trapped in a pine box in the middle of Iraq or lost on a deserted island, as authors of singular perspective stories, you have to look within the drama of human emotion rather than finding existential threats. If your character is lost, in addition to the natural danger that being lost presents, there are also the psychological challenges the character would go through. A while back I was shooting some interview material with a man who had spent most of his adult life in solitary confinement. Arrested in his early twenties, the man had recently been released from prison at the age of thirty-seven. He talked about the struggle he had to not go crazy and how he had to use his solitude in a productive way in order to survive. He wrote music and beats. Over the course of his incarceration, he smuggled recording equipment into his cell, where he created music and self-published it. Every time he was caught doing this by prison staff, they would throw him back in the hole. Ultimately, this man was released, and he went on to creating a huge following through his music, and he is now doing some positive things with his life.

What I found so fascinating about this story was that one man, separated by the horrors of day-to-day prison life, safe from the general population, safe from all the existential threats we associate with being incarcerated, had to face the worst danger of all: going insane.

For me, this story only solidifies the notion that there is so much more to the human conflict than the monster, or the storm. Your mind is really your tinderbox, and you can use that as a trap for your characters. This allows you, once again, to compress the need for multiple characters, locations, or dialogue.

Chapter 9:

How to Run Your Set

Keeping Your Set Tiny

By nature, filmmaking is a community experience. It is also a workplace that requires specialists and experienced crew labor; that is unavoidable. The real trick with microbudget filmmaking is navigating the needs, the "absolutes," with the wants, the "it-would-be-nice-to-haves." Under no circumstance should you ever cut back labor when it comes to crew safety, although in recent times, the risk of pandemics like COVID-19 has pushed the industry to minimize its crew sizes to avoid the spread of infectious diseases.

Before working on this book, I visited a set where I noticed the production had nearly twenty-five people working on it. On a surface level, it appeared like a well-oiled machine, and by the looks of it, it seemed like the filmmakers had a decent budget to facilitate all of those folks. However, shortly after they wrapped, the producers acknowledged two vitally important stressors that had handicapped their operations. One was catering. In addition to the dozen or so crew people, they also had actors, actors' friends, and other lookie loos who ate their way through their wallets. Additionally, the producing team secretly grumbled about the speed at which they were moving. It was a snail's pace, and the setups were taking much longer because people were in one another's ways.

The producers had only employed two-thirds of the staff on set. The rest were volunteers from a local film program. In the first few days, it was exciting to have a community of people involved, but as the weeks progressed, the volume of bodies became a liability. Ultimately, the production completed, but it left the filmmakers with an overbudget deficit and some explaining to do with investors.

The moral of this tale is very simple: fewer bodies on set equals less liability. Now, this being said, you still need people to staff various departments. However, be sure there are no areas where you have extra people for the sake of extra people. Moreover, you are personally responsible for all of the people on your set. If someone gets hurt, regardless of whether they are a volunteer or not, you will have to answer for that, one way or another. Be sure to keep your head count small!

Depending on the type of movie you are making, you could also be forced to add more staff or volunteers to the equation. Make sure you factor that in when developing. Remember, the goal of this book is to help you produce a microbudget movie ($30,000–$60,000). Action films will require more staff than a comedy. Sci-fi films may require more people than an action film, and so forth. If you have a particular stunt or visual effect, then you should anticipate more staff. Plus, if you are working on a union set, you may be required to have a certain staff level for various jobs such as transportation, camera, grip/electric, and catering.

Union versus Nonunion

Safety and health should never be overlooked when it comes to a movie or TV production. This especially is true when it comes to food, craft services, stunts, weapons safety, medical staff, and rigging. Moreover, it is true that you get what you pay for. There are major benefits to hiring seasoned crew persons and working with unions. However, if you do decide to go nonunion for your crew, make sure you are finding experienced workers who can facilitate the demands of the job. Be sure to hire people who are above the level of a professional.

Overspending in Filmmaking

I have been on many sets over the years (both big and small) and have discovered a wide spectrum of overspending. Most of a set's overspending is with labor. I have directed commercial shoots where clients insisted on bulking up the crew just to impress their stakeholders. Most of the time, you can do the job with fewer people. I have also seen indie film sets with dozens of volunteer crew people bumping into each other and eating their way through catering budgets. When you are making a microbudget film, your margin of error on budget is so thin that one extra sandwich could put you in the red! This is why it is important to take inventory on the areas of labor that are needed and reduce the parts that can be consolidated.

From a filmmaking mindset perspective, direct your mind toward the aspects of efficiency when thinking of your crew. Only have the staff you need. Keep your sets closed. Resist the need for your talent's entourage or any additional bodies on set that will slow you down.

Communicate and Set Aside Your Ego

Every department supervisor loves to have lots of minions under them. Some calls are necessary, while other areas are not. Many crew members are unaware of the financial challenges movies face. It is your responsibility to bring your budgetary challenges to your crew early on in preproduction and allow them to help you find solutions to reducing crew expenses. It is also vitally important for you to listen to your team and take advice. You will most certainly have to make compromises to some of your plans, just like a department supervisor would have to compromise, having to work harder or longer hours to accommodate your tiny budget. It is up to both of you to

117

find solutions that are manageable and safe. Furthermore, it is important to always remember that once the script leaves your head and goes into production, it is a manufacturing product. Don't take compromise personally. Set aside your artistic ego, and listen to your team!

Think like a Documentary Crew

When my company and I produce movies, we do so with roughly nine people on staff. The rest are day hires brought in when needed. Obviously, some scenes will require more crew and cast in general, but I design scripts to function at this level.

We shoot most of our feature films nonunion in Nevada and have worked with the same team for years. These people are like family, and we enjoy making films together. Our team has learned to work at a high level with less. We manage to maintain professionalism, safety, and quality despite our crew size. Most of us wear multiple hats, and we shoot our features like we would a documentary or reality TV show. *But again, our ability to do this is in the design of the script and production plan.*

Here is a list of my regular staff:

1. Director / producer / location manager (me)
2. Camera operator / director of photography
3. Camera assistant / media manager
4. Assistant director / script supervisor
5. Grip person / gaffer / rigger
6. Sound person
7. Props / safety person
8. Catering person
9. Makeup, hair and wardrobe person
10. Production assistants / slate (varies, depending on demand)

   Occasional hires:

1. Stuntpeople
2. Production drivers
3. Police / security / weapons handling
4. Special costumes
5. More grips
6. Drone pilot (FAA approved)
7. Animal handlers
8. Underwater photographers
9. Visual effects supervisor

The Movie Is Made in Preproduction

I have lectured on the importance of preproduction for years, and I truly believe a movie is made in preproduction. Preproduction is the brains, heart, and soul of a film project. If preproduction is not complete, or is half-assed or rushed, then the movie suffers, the crew suffers, and ultimately, your wallet suffers.

Most of the job functions that are needed for preproduction such as budgeting, shot lists, location management, casting, set design, wardrobe, and props are areas that my wife and I manage prior to principal photography. We wear multiple hats leading into production. It is always our goal to close down each of those back-office production duties before we put on our production hats.

Take time to find your locations, cast and workshop your actors, break down shot lists with your camera people, and take care of any other duties that you need before filming. Racing into production is a huge mistake, no matter the reason. Be patient, and do as many of the back-end tasks as possible before getting to set. Once you are on set, the clock starts ticking, and money starts burning!

Take a Small Business Course

In order for a filmmaker to maintain quality on his or her set, one must learn to do things themselves. It is always my recommendation to take a small business class somewhere before starting your production. As the chief operating officer, secretary, and treasurer of your project, you must understand basic administrative functions and know how to manage a workplace. One of the biggest handicaps I see with indie productions is that rarely anyone at the top has taken a business course or has managed people outside of a production environment.

The DIY Filmmaker

Although filmmaking is a community sport, it also requires its leaders to understand every aspect of the industry. *The job of an indie filmmaker is to be able to perform all tasks on a motion picture production, and lead by example and with integrity.* You must know how to use a camera and change a lens. You must understand and know how to make a shot list, set up lights, and work a camera dolly. You must know how to schedule, make call sheets, run human resources, hire people, and know basic state and federal workplace safety guidelines. You should know editing, sound design, and color correction. You should know basic graphic design and social media marketing. Sound overwhelming? Well, it is. That is why preproduction is more important than principal photography!

Working with Your Limitations

I will stress this point again: it is of keen importance to know your limitations when making a movie and design your production to work within these limitations. Take inventory in what you already have, and try to craft something around it.

For example, if you live in rural Virginia, you should not be aiming to make a microbudget movie set in New York City. If you live in the deserts of the southwest United States, don't try to make a movie about the Vietnam

War in your backyard. Use what you have, and pull from that. Find inspiration where you stand, and aim to make a quality product with the limited resources you have. It is a challenge, yes, but the process can be widely fulfilling!

Chapter 10:

Building Your Distribution Plan

Many filmmakers have the false idea that once you sign a distribution agreement, somehow your movie will magically start making money. Even worse, producers make the mistake of thinking that once their film is released by a distributor, they can sit back, relax, and collect checks. Distribution is really the beginning of your filmmaking enterprise. Once you sign the deal or hit the publish button, it's go time!

As your film is released, it is typically up to you to help the distributor promote and mobilize the product. A sales company can sell your work or secure a VOD platform for your movie, but it's up to you to carry the marketing drum. There is a big misunderstanding as to what film distributors and sales agents actually do. Oftentimes, it's wrongly assumed that distributors will market your film. Typically, the marketing extent most companies will perform is to take your movie to various trade shows, create a poster and trailer for the movie, and list your film in their catalog.

Most indie distributors will not spend money on airing your trailer on TV, publishing spots in magazines, or even running ads on social media. The main reason for this is that they do not need to, and the cost to do so would not make sense. In fact, the average cost of marketing would more than likely exceed the budget that it cost to make the movie.

Moreover, from the distributor's perspective, their audience is not the general public. Their audience comprises film buyers. They usually focus on acquiring movies that create sales at the market. That said, there are a few companies that do champion various movies, but those titles are films that can help bolster their own prestige. If your movie won a jury prize at Cannes or Sundance, they most likely would advertise those points outside their norm. Aside from that, the average filmmaker is generally left with the responsibility to push his or her own content.

So Why Have a Distributor?

There is a growing movement of filmmakers who are making the shift away from the traditional distribution model. Creatives are finding self-distribution more sensible. With the advent of aggregators (companies you hire to release your movie across multiple platforms), and the world still reeling from the greatest crisis in modern history, one could make the argument that indie filmmakers no longer need traditional distributors and sales companies. However, the world is still a big place, and there are several ways in which filmmakers can benefit from some of the traditional models. The way I look at it is a multipronged approach.

The final chapter of the book is dedicated to giving you two scenarios that can be merged into one plan for releasing your film. Regardless of whether you are signing with a traditional sales company or releasing your movie yourself, a distribution plan should give rigorous thought to audience demographics. Your plan should include the following:

1. Social media ad targeting
2. The timing of release
3. Which distribution rights you will keep or split with a distributor

In most cases, I do a rights split with my distribution partner. This means that I keep some of my video on demand rights domestically for self-distribution while allowing my distributor to sell the movie internationally to certain platforms. As a result, I must always think about coordinating the release with the distributor to maximize audience engagement. This model is a partnership with the distributor.

Long-Term Strategy

It typically takes me a year or two to completely recoup my investments and start seeing an ROI. It takes time for a movie to make it into the market, find its audience, and start earning. Patience is a virtue one must have when venturing into distribution. Your strategy should always be long term! If you are looking to make a quick buck, go into some other type of business.

Building Your Library

Think of your movie making like building a collection of books. The more books you have, the more impressive your library is. Moreover, having multiple movies in your library is the most effective way to earn returns from your work long term. Movies can also cross-promote each other.

It has always been my long-term strategy to build up a library of media. It has offered ongoing residual income benefits for my company and crew. I have achieved this by producing in genres that are evergreen. I also keep my investment into projects very low. It is also important that we make sure our movies look and sound as professional as possible. Putting out garbage won't help.

I typically slice up my content rights like a pizza pie. I divide them up between my distribution partner and my own company. Usually, I give the distributor control over areas that are more challenging for my team to reach ourselves, like international markets. However, we maintain certain domestic rights, which are easily managed through aggregators and self-publishing tools. This gives my team the ability to control our brand more and monetize certain aspects of the film that does not require profit splits with the sales company.

Through our distributor partner, we sell movies in places that would normally be unreachable with self-publishing tools. This includes international VOD outlets, major brick-and-mortar retailers, and overseas broadcast outlets. Because of our distributor, our content sits on the same shelves as major studio movies and shares the same market potential as any film released. This level of release helps other parts of our business in ways separate from the movie itself. It adds prestige for our small studio and credibility with our service clients, and it helps market other aspects of our business around the world.

Self-Publishing Your Film

Today there are dozens of ways a filmmaker can self-distribute their content. The question is no longer "Can a filmmaker find distribution?" but rather "Can a filmmaker find a market for their content?" Simply publishing your titles to YouTube, Amazon, iTunes, Vimeo, or any of the other VOD outlets does not guarantee you will find a market.

Your distribution strategy should focus on the following phases of release:

1. **Narrow down where your target audience mostly shops.** Do some market research. If your audience typically comprises video gamers, then aim for platforms that may be available on gaming platforms. If your film is designed for horror audiences, maybe find platforms that are geared toward that audience.

2. **Build your social media and engagement.** Marketing these days is more than simply running ads or commercials. Marketing calls for engagement. To do this, look at social media platforms as your biggest tool. Create user forums, and call for interaction with your audience. Making your audience feel that they have some investment

in the product will help your self-distribution efforts dramatically. Investigate and research how other filmmakers are doing this, and create your own plan.

3. **Timing your release.** Timing your release is important. You must consider the excitement factor and give time for your audience to build that level of enthusiasm. Create scheduled social media posts and count down the release as if it's the most important thing in the universe.

4. **Title matters.** I know that titles of movies are touchy subjects with filmmakers, but think of your title as your single most important marketing tool. Titles should always reflect the theme (if possible) or contain a searchable keyword that can help people discover you easier. If your movie is about service animals, try implementing that search word into your title. Oftentimes, filmmakers try to get too clever with naming their little microbudget movies. This can relegate you to the shelves of obscurity. Unless you have money to spend marketing your

title, you should consider creating easy-to-find titles that people will accidently find when searching for other things.

5. **Artwork must look legit.** In basic speak, your title should look like it's a studio film. As mentioned previously, your art should look clean and contemporary. Do some homework, and don't be afraid to draw from other films for inspiration. Don't steal or copy stuff, but look at how the poster is laid out. Look at what types of fonts they used and what information they presented. Studios have paid millions in market testing and research to figure these things out. Why not take advantage of the free lesson?

6. **Mobilize your audience.** The most critical time for any movie release is the first twenty-four hours. Your main goal for your film's initial release is to mobilize your audience to watch your movie within the first day of its initial release. Doing so helps search engines populate your title based on relevancy, and in some cases, this can place your

film at the top of categories. The "trickling viewership effect" doesn't work. You need to aim for an initial surge of views on your content when it is fresh.

Working with Distributors

In my book, *What Film Schools Don't Tell You*, I outline several aspects of working with a distributor. These include how to negotiate the best deal for yourself. It also contains a step-by-step process of how things go with working with a distributor, from the time you send your first query letter and beyond. I will spare readers that detailed information in this chapter and get right to the most important points of the subject.

What Types of Traditional Deals to Sign

The term *gross* is a term that you should have tattooed on the back of your hand as a reminder. *You should only sign gross deals with no expenses.* Expense deals are horrible for the microbudget filmmaker, who has little leverage outside of the film itself. A gross deal refers to a contract in which the distributor cannot add any expenses to the receipts for money they collect. If they make money, you make money. Now, this being said, you may have to negotiate a lower percentage split with the sales company, but having a lower percentage on revenue is still better than an expense deal. You would be better signing away 60 percent of your profit rights for a gross deal rather than keeping 80 percent of your net revenue income.

Gross deals are better for filmmakers because it is entirely uncertain what types of expenses a company will put on your film. Even with an expense cap, films rarely make profits with these deals. For example, let's say you signed a net deal with an expense cap of $30,000. This scenario would mean your movie would have to make $30,000 first before you would start earning a nickel. The first $30,000 would go straight into the distributor's pocket, which they will justify by saying it costs them $30,000 to market and promote your film. Rubbish!

Most sales companies and distributors will spend less than $2,000 to market a microbudget feature, outside of whatever the cost to travel to various film markets. Oftentimes, distribution companies and sales agencies will try to pass the expense costs of attending various markets to their clients. If you think about it, it's a complete rip-off, because they would be attending film markets regardless of whether your film was in their catalog or not. And even worse, some predatory companies will try to pass the entire cost of the trade show to be a single film title!

By the time most microbudget films hit the $30,000 revenue threshold, it has been at least a year or so after the distribution agreement has been signed. Sadly, by the time you are finally in a position to make money on your film, the distributor has moved on and is now pushing dozens of new titles at trade shows and film markets. Your movie is officially old and is placed in the hospice of filmmaking, slowly and painfully waiting out the term of its contract.

The Answer

To be better positioned to make revenue back for your film, it is vitally important that you make money immediately after your film hits the market. You can only achieve this by signing a gross revenue deal. You can negotiate this position by asking for a lower percentage of gross. You may have to offer up some other concession like cutting your own trailer, making your own artwork, or even placing ads on social media at your expense. Be creative, and always know that if a company isn't willing to budge on a gross deal, they are more than likely a bad company for you anyway. Do not be afraid to walk away from that deal!

Definition of Gross Receipts

When working on a deal that involves *gross receipts*, be sure to ask your legal counsel to include any definitions of gross revenues. Make sure that there is no revenue that could be taxed with distribution or any other hidden fees. It is also to include any revenue from third-party deals. This includes any and all moneys derived from the exploitation of your motion picture.

Keep Your Ancillary Rights

When signing a blanket agreement, many companies will want to own all of your rights to your movie. This includes sequels, books, movie titles, comics, stories, and adaptation rights. The distribution company does not need these rights, so be sure to have them removed from your agreement before signing.

Short-Term Agreement

The average term limit should be between three and five years. It typically takes a movie a year to get into the market and start earning money. However, I have seen some agreements that ask for ten years or more! These are bad situations to be in. Contracts are hard enough to get out of once a distributor starts executing their rights, so having shorter term limits will minimize the risk long term.

Get a Real Entertainment Lawyer

Lastly, you should always consult with the appropriate legal professional before signing any distribution deal or film-related agreement. There may be pitfalls within an agreement that you cannot see. A trained entertainment law professional who has experience looking at distribution contracts should be retained.

When you are looking for a lawyer, find someone who has experience dealing with distribution contracts. Not all entertainment lawyers are the same. Hiring a lawyer who deals with tap dancers won't help you. Find someone who has experience working in indie film rights management. When interviewing prospective lawyers, be sure to ask them if they have worked in movie distribution and contract negotiation.

It is also important that you tell your lawyer what terms you wish to see implemented into your agreement. You cannot assume they will have the previous points in mind. Most lawyers are primarily focused on mitigating your risk in a contract. It is crucial that you ask them to help you position a profitable deal.

Film Distribution Plans

As we start to wrap up the final chapter of this book, I will present two options for you. Both of these options are designed for the microbudget filmmaker who has a movie that costs $60,000 or less. These two options can be combined into one strategy and used as a multipronged approach to releasing your movie.

Distribution Plan 1: Self-Release

As mentioned in the beginning of this chapter, there are several things to consider when choosing to self-publish your film. However, here are a few steps to plan for.

1. **Step one:** Start your marketing efforts early. Don't wait for the film to be finished or even to start shooting. Start the marketing process the second you decide to make your movie. If it's too late for that, find ways to create conversations for your audience via social media. Deputize your cast and

crew, and have them help you create these conversations.

2. **Step two:** Plan out your release date. Look for timeframes for your release that will service your film and its genre. For example, if you have a children's movie, try releasing it over the summer when kids are out of school. If you have a Christmas movie, release it directly after Thanksgiving. Try your best to be thoughtful for the timing of your release, and make sure you give yourself plenty of time to promote and build up excitement.

3. **Step three:** Plan the platforms your movie will be on first. Try not to release your film to multiple platforms all at once. Release your film in phases. Try to focus your marketing efforts to promote each platform exclusively, and do not overextend yourself.

4. **Step four:** Rinse and repeat. Just because your film is released, it does *not* mean it is time to hang up your hat. In fact, your real work has begun. You

should start looking at creative ways to keep the conversation and excitement of your movie going. You could even use film festivals as marketing opportunities to promote your film's ongoing release.

5. **Step five:** Market your own personal services. The movie is only one aspect of your career. You should always think about how to use your movie as a marketing piece to push your career with other things. If you are a professional video editor, then you should consider marketing yourself as such by using your film as a platform to talk about these things. Making your own movie is an excellent way to market yourself as an actor, director, writer, editor, and even video production pro.

6. **Step six:** Make sure your title and artwork are in line with the previous section on self-releasing. A strong, search-friendly title and eye-catching artwork can help your title on VOD platforms in more ways than spending money running ads.

Distribution Plan 2: Traditional Distribution

In effort to maximize your film's potential, you may consider working with a traditional distribution company for your release. Unlike aggregators (companies that you pay to place you on multiple platforms, and you retain your rights), distribution companies have access to buyers in places across the globe. But before you sign, think about these following steps.

1. **Step one:** Start the conversation early with a potential distribution company. Oftentimes, filmmakers think they have to wait to have a film before contacting distributors. False. As you develop your screenplay, try creating a distribution conversation. Contact companies and see if they would be interested in reviewing your early material, with hopes (of course) of distributing the film once it's complete. I start this conversation by asking companies if they would be willing to offer any advice on the material to make it better suited for their catalog. While there may be a few

companies that will tell you to piss off, you would be surprised by how many folks are willing to give you their opinions on things. Again, the goal here is to start creating a conversation about your film and planning to build a relationship with a distribution partner.

2. **Step two:** Once you sign a distribution agreement, start working closely with the company to help promote various releases. This keeps engagement moving and relationships strong. You should also consider helping them promote other titles in their catalog.

3. **Step three:** Start developing new content with your distributor. This may seem premature, but having a strong relationship with your sales company is an opportunity to think of the future. Whether your movie is a classic scripted narrative or a documentary, keeping the future in play is important to your career.

4. **Step four:** Be patient. One of the biggest challenges in working with a distributor is being patient. It

takes time to make things happen. Be patient, and use this time to build a long-term relationship with your distributor or sales agency.

As I conclude this chapter, I will stress one last point on distribution: please make distribution the foremost important part of your business plan. Do not leave distribution to chance. Take time at becoming an expert on this area of filmmaking, and ask for help when you need it. There is no greater tragedy to the filmmaking experience than seeing a filmmaker create a movie only for it to be lost to bad distribution planning. Make it the most important part of your job. Moneymaking may not be the most important thing to you while making your movie, but without thinking of distribution, you might as well make home movies for your family. No one will really see your content.

Epilogue:

A New Mindset

In March 2020, the entire world lay witness to one of the most horrific pandemics the world has seen in a hundred years. It also was a major economic blow to the entertainment industry. Due to the tragic COVID-19 pandemic, the greatest companies in our industry became huge financial liabilities overnight and were completely paralyzed within a flash. Movie theaters shuttered across the globe, event venues and theme parks closed indefinitely, and the strategy for production and distribution changed forever. Stakeholders at all the major studios started asking themselves the hard questions on budgets and started scrambling to find new ways to produce content in an era without the power of the box office.

What the 2020 pandemic showed Hollywood was that movies were costing too much to produce. In a market that would now demand higher quantities of product and speed, the "multimillion-dollar movie" suddenly came into question. With the industry having to rely primarily on streaming platforms to monetize content, producers started asking how they could make more content for less. Overnight, smaller budget movies and TV shows seemed to get people's attention.

No True Rules

Over the course of my twenty-plus-year career as a filmmaker, I have discovered one thing. There are no true rules to making films, and there is no secret sauce that goes into being successful. Success in the business can only be measured by one's endurance in the sport.

What the Future Demands

In today's industry, the most rewarding pathway to becoming a film director, producer, or screenwriter is through the lens of microbudget filmmaking. It is the one area of the industry that any person can build their talent, gain exposure, and find their voice. Best of all, a person can do this without creating a financial calamity for themselves or others. This brave new world of filmmaking now requires new thinkers, new stories, and a demand for creatives that can do more with less.

It is without question that the world as we once knew it has fundamentally changed over the past decade and will continue to evolve. In fact, when I started writing this book, I had never even heard of COVID-19. By the time I finished this epilogue, the global pandemic had crippled economies all over the world and caused thousands upon thousands of deaths and endless suffering. It has changed our industry forever and has caused even the greatest players in our business to shutter and go to war with one another. The old way of doing business has changed, and it is an opportunity to grow in new ways and learn.

As I look toward the future, I can only suggest to my readers that you look at your career anew. Think differently about how you create your films and how you build your business. In this great time of change, it is so important to be resourceful and smart about the things that you develop. Developing with purpose is key. My greatest mission with any of my teachings is to inspire hope and self-confidence and to encourage those of you who wish to make movies to do so with purpose.

I started from nothing. I had little education and financial means when I got into this business, but I have managed to make myself into something positive. I can honestly say I am proud of my company and the team that we have built. I know that you can do the same for yourself.

The concept of thinking smaller may fly in the face of industry norms, considering that the business of motion picture is all about the big and epic. However, if you wait around too long trying to break into Hollywood, you may spend the rest of your life waiting to make movies. I know a lot of people like this. This is the reason why it is so important for me to help aspiring filmmakers understand that the Hollywood dream most of us grew up with lives within us, not in some far-off place.

Today the market is largely global and demands a pragmatic and straightforward approach to creating new content. Costs of production have skyrocketed over the last few decades. The demand for ROI is so crucial that studios and television providers are looking for new alternative ways to create content and keep costs low. This new world of content creating has been driven by finite audience targeting and branded content. There is a bright and vibrant world of independent filmmaking yet to be conquered, and the time to think differently is now! *Think with a filmmaking mindset!*

References

Films

- *Abigail Haunting (Motion Picture 2020) Kelly Schwarze*
- *Alien Domicile (Motion Picture 2017) Kelly Schwarze*
- *All is Lost (Motion Picture 2013) J. C. Chandor*
- *Fog City Mavericks (Documentary 2007) Gary Leva*
- *One Cut of the Dead (Motion Picture 2017) Shinichiro Ueda*
- *Walt: The Man Behind the Myth (Documentary 2001) Jean-Pierre Isbouts*

Online Resources

- *Biography.com*
- *en.wikipedia.org*
- *notablebiographies.com*
- *oprah.com*
- *quoteswave.com*

<u>Books</u>

- *Rebel Without A Crew by Robert Rodriguez*
- *The Movie Business: The Definitive Guide to the Legal and Financial Secrets of Getting Your Movie Made by Kelly Charles Crab*

- *The Visual Mindscape of the Screenplay by Bill Boyle*
- *Walt Disney: The Triumph of the American Imagination by Neal Gabler (2007)*
- *What Film Schools Don't Tell You: Your Basic Guide to Making Movies and Finding Good Distribution by Kelly Schwarze*

A FILMMAKING

MINDSET

THE NEW PATH OF TODAY'S FILMMAKER

JOIN OUR FILMMAKING COMMUNITY

www.indiefilmfactory.com

@iffactory

facebook.com/indiefilmfactory.com

Made in the USA
Las Vegas, NV
11 October 2023

78932405R00100